Ad'Mat

Using the 25 Classic Advertising Formats

Michael Klassen • Robb Klassen
Michael J. McAnally • Cindy L. Hunting

Kendall Hunt
publishing company

Kendall Hunt
publishing company

www.kendallhunt.com
Send all inquiries to:
4050 Westmark Drive
Dubuque, IA 52004-1840

Copyright © 2009 by Kendall Hunt Publishing Company

ISBN 978-0-7575-6568-7

Printed in the United States of America
10 9 8 7 6 5 4 3 2

Contents

Preface

"Necessity is the mother of invention."

This book was born out of a need. There simply is no book to date that explains in the kind of detail seen here the most used advertising formats in the business.

What do you get? Simply, you get an exhaustive explanation of the 25 most used formats in advertising. Each of the 20 chapters follows the same structure: a short description of each format is followed by an explanation of when advertisers may use and should not use it. Each chapter also offers insights into how the format should be executed, including a suggested balance ratio of copy to visual elements and suggestions on how these may be positioned in the ad field. Finally, a list of media that are acceptable or not acceptable venues for the format is included to help you place your advertisement: print, outdoor, metro, direct, fax, home page, landing page, counter-topper, insert, or card. Your understanding is enhanced by an actual advertisement created by the authors solely to demonstrate the format, permitting you to verbally and visually understand each one.

Have there been other formats? Yes. One need only look, as have the authors, at ads from days gone by, from the 1920s, the 30s, the 40s, and dozens of different formats can be identified. But it is only a handful, 25 to be exact, that have stood the test of time. Here these 25 formats are explained by an advertising professor and consultant (Michael L. Klassen, Ph.D.) who has spent countless hours educating and consulting on advertising format with hundreds of students and clients. And not just explained. Acting as creative director of a very young team, Klassen is assisted in the visual explanation of these formats by two young professionals-marketing/graphic design students Mike McAnally and Cindy Hunting-and a single commercial photographer, Robb Graber Klassen, a student at the world's premier advertising photography school, the renowned Brooks Institute.

How do educators stand to benefit from reading and using this book? For advertising and marketing educators, no more searching through last week's Vogue or Newsweek trying to find class examples; no more hastily constructed PowerPoint presentations that ultimately fall short of a full rendering of the strengths, weaknesses, uses, and construction of these essential layouts-just pull examples from the book, or better yet, assign the book, assured that it will be a valuable resource your advertising and marketing students will use for the rest of their professional lives.

And how may creative directors and advertising professionals benefit? For them, no more tedious explanations to the creative team-just give them this book with the desired formats marked and tell them to get to work. And for business owners long on imagination but short on cash, no more believing that in order to create a good print ad, design a new home page, or to just put together a simple but compelling table-topper, insert, card, brochure, or landing page they have to hire a $100-an-hour designer.

Complete with a glossary and training assignments, this book has all any advertising professional-educator or practitioner-needs to explain, understand, and execute professional layout and design. One book alone and you can consider your library on this extremely important aspect of advertising implementation to be complete.

About the Authors

MIKE KLASSEN (Creative Director, Writer) received his Ph.D. in cognitive psychology in 1987 and, that same year, became a marketing professor specializing in advertising and consumer behavior. He has published over fifty articles and three books and has spoken to audiences in Europe, Asia, and South America. He was Invited Professor at Jordan, McGrath, Case, & Taylor Advertising in New York and has consulted with businesses nationwide. His research has been featured on ABC 20/20 and NBC News Magazine - Europe/Asia, and he has appeared on Dateline NBC. He lives with his wife, Emily, in Cedar Falls, Iowa where he teaches at the University of Northern Iowa. They have three grown children: Scott, Robb, and Jeni.

MICHAEL MCANALLY (Graphic Designer) graduated from the University of Northern Iowa with a Bachelors degree in Marketing. Michael also developed his skills in Graphic Design, Web Design, and Internet Marketing. Michael is currently working on a Masters degree in International Marketing at ESC Rennes School of Business in Rennes, France.

ROBB KLASSEN (Photographer) is a student at Brooks Institute in Santa Barbara, California, the premier advertising photography school in the nation. He had his first photography show at age 15 in Iowa City, Iowa. He has had his photographs published multiple times in the *North American Review*. Robb's photography includes: product, architectural, travel, fashion, and portraiture. This is his first book. Robb lives at the base of the Santa Ynez Mountains and is an avid rock climber.

CINDY L. HUNTING (Graphic Designer) graduated from the University of Northern Iowa with a bachelor's degree with an emphasis in marketing, sales and advertising, and graphic communications. While interning for an advertising agency, she refined her skills in communication, graphic design, Web design, and print design. Cindy lives in Ankeny, Iowa and enjoys spending her free time designing, scrapbooking, cooking, and spending time with her friends, family, and boyfriend.

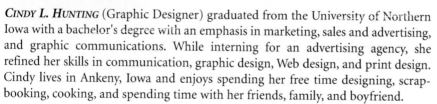

Ad'Mat

Using the 25 Classic Advertising Formats

The Standard Format

FLEXIBLE AND DEPENDABLE PRINT ADVERTISING LAYOUT

Description:

The standard format is one of the oldest and most used formats-offering as it does a layout that will accommodate the advertising of a wide berth of products, services, and ideas. This format uses strong visual and verbal stimuli to grab attention, increase comprehension, and spur action. Part of its appeal is the fact that the standard format is relatively easy to construct, even for the amateur advertiser. Unlike with some other formats, the advertiser is able to include a substantial variety of visual and verbal information about the product and the consumer benefits of using it.

When Used:

Simple but not simplistic, the standard format is used for products sold on Main Street and Fifth Avenue; for consumer and industrial products; and for organizational, service, idea, and event advertising. Advertisers use the standard format when they believe they have either strong headline or compelling product images (headline is often written in black blocky letters against a white background.) One or the other of these (headline or image) is positioned in the top portion of the advertisement where it is the first thing seen by the consumer. The standard format is also used when advertisers believe they have strong body copy to pull the viewer into the ad and increase her/his understanding of the key benefit and central promise. Finally, advertisers may use the standard format when they offer an exceptional price, which is usually boxed and placed in either the bottom right- or left-hand corner of the advertisement. If the visual does not include the brand or logo, advertisers typically include a small pack shot in either the bottom right- or left-hand corner.

Copy/Image Balance and Execution:

The standard format is highly predictable in balance and composition. The top 55-60% of the ad field is reserved for either image or headline. If the top is filled with a visual image, the headline appears directly beneath it as a horizontal bar taking up approximately 10-15% of the ad field. Directly beneath the headline will appear body copy (approximately 20% of the field) in either two or three vertical columns. The bottom left- or right-hand corner of the ad field is reserved for a pack shot (if the visual in the top half is not branded) and/or a boxed price. If the top is filled with headline, the area beneath will be reserved for columns of body copy with a generous portion of the ad field left over for a product shot or branded pack shot. A boxed price may appear in either bottom corner of the ad field.

Media Used:

The standard format has defined decades of excellent print advertising, especially magazine advertising. It is too crowded and dense for outdoor, metro, cards, and brochures. It can work for counter-toppers, fax, landing pages, Website home pages, and inserts.

"The best sounding table radio ever made." (MSNBC)

The Tivol Audio Model One AM/FM Table Radio

With a tuner that brings clarity to many of the weakest stations, the Model One radio begins with a handmade wood cabinet that is both beautiful and the ideal acoustically inert speaker housing. A heavy-magnet, long-throw driver is mated to a frequency contouring circuit that automatically adjusts output over half-octave increments, resulting in musically accurate tonal balance and bass response.

Like all Tivol Audio products, the Model One AM/FM table radio is compatible with iPod and other players. Available in five finishes, for yourself or someone else you care about.

Tivol Audio

The Grid Format
STRONG AND MEMORABLE

Description:

The grid format is a modified version of the standard format using compelling visual stimuli and verbal content to create a highly balanced and symmetrical layout through the use of four equilateral squares. Each square becomes a "framed masterpiece," showcasing strong visual images of the product, the company plant, employees, customers, etc. The grid format may be attributed to Andy Warhol's 1962 piece (seen below) titled Campbell's Soup Cans, which appears on 32 separate panels. As reflected in Warhol's work, the grid format presents stimuli in a manner that makes an impact, is focused, and is attention-getting. The symmetry of the grid format makes it particularly useful in creating a serious tone.

When Used:

Advertisers use the grid format when they have access to four compelling images, or alternatively, if four images don't exist, the designer can multiply a single compelling image four times and position each in its own square. A distinctive touch (again, à la Mr. Warhol, as seen below in his piece, Marilyn Monroe) is employed by the advertiser who uses the same image four times in different shades and colors.

Copy/Image Balance and Execution:

Like the standard format, the grid format uses the top half (no less than 55%) of the ad field to present visual information, in this case, in four squares. What lies directly beneath in a horizontal bar (10-15% of the ad field) is a headline followed by two or three columns of vertical body copy (approximately 20% of the ad field). The bottom left- or right-hand corner of the advertisement is reserved for a pack shot if the featured visuals do not have a branded image of the product. The advertiser may also include a boxed price if desired.

© Andy Warhol Foundation/Corbis.

Media Used:

The grid format is an excellent format for magazines. Especially when the featured visual is repetitive, this format also works for outdoor and metro if the copy is left to a bare minimum. The grid format can be used to create an attractive card, brochure, insert, fax, Web home page, counter-topper, and landing page

© Andy Rain/epa/Corbis.

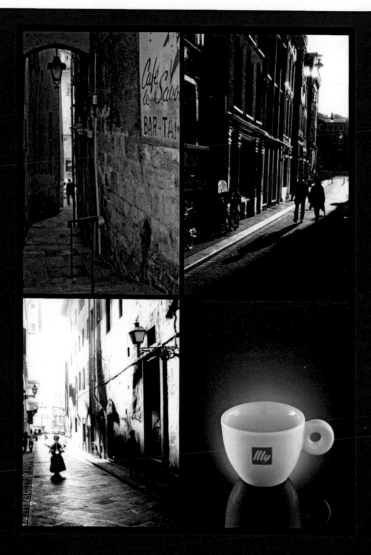

For over 70 years the good citizens
of Trieste in northern Italy
have started their day with Illy.

Now its *your* turn.

Illyusa.com

The Frame Format

FORMAL/INFORMAL INTERCHANGEABILITY

Description:

The frame format uses either copy or visual images to frame, and thereby focus attention on, the central promise made by the advertiser or the key consumer benefit offered. They are interchangeable: sometimes images frame verbal copy and sometimes verbal copy frames images. The choice is made according to the advertiser's judgments based on which (what is said or what is pictured) is most compelling. This format thereby gives advertisers some flexibility, allowing them to choose their strongest suit (i.e., if the image is weak, they can still fall back on copy, and vice versa).

When Used:

The frame format can be used to express formality or informality. When advertisers wish to communicate a sense of fun, lightheartedness, and enjoyment, they use images to frame copy. When advertisers desire to express formality, they use copy to frame images. Why? When copy is used as a frame, it enhances and adds definition to the angular element of the ad border thus contributing a formal and symmetrical sense to the advertisement. Because images are rarely angular and symmetrical, framing with images creates asymmetry that increases the informality of the composition, often adding a sense of enjoyment and, even, frivolity.

Copy/Image Balance and Execution:

The copy-to-image ratio in the frame format is roughly the same. Together they may constitute as much as 80% of the ad field, leaving ample room for other copy and image, such as branding, headline, price, pack shot, and legally required information.

Media Used:

The frame is often used in restaurant advertising to create counter-toppers, menus, cards, and posters. It may be used in magazines, newspapers, fax, Web home pages, landing pages, and inserts. The frame format is often too visually busy for outdoor and metro advertising.

Jacob's Platter
SANTA BARBARA
Dinner tonight was harvested
from the Santa Ynez
Valley this morning.

Taste the local difference.

The Gaze Format
MODEL AS DIRECTIONAL CUE

Description:

The gaze format uses a human model to direct the viewer's attention to the object of attention, which may include a special price, the brand, the product itself, the central promise made by the advertiser, the consumer benefit, a pack shot, and much more. The gaze format draws attention to the object by posing the model so that she/he looks at or gestures toward it.

When Used:

The gaze format is used with either photographed or illustrated models to visually steer the viewer in a predetermined direction. As such, it is a type of pointing device that is used when the advertiser believes that the object of attention by itself does not possess the desired attention-getting power.

Copy/Image Balance and Execution:

With the gaze format, the position of the model and how much ad field is devoted to the model is governed by a single question: "Does the model's gaze move the viewer in the desired direction?" If the image of the model is visually compelling by itself, it is given ample space to serve its function as a pointing device. It is important to understand, however, that the "star" of any advertisement is always and only the product, not the model. Therefore, the model should never overshadow the intended object of attention.

Media Used:

The gaze format is very flexible and may be used in variety of media, including: magazines, newspapers, outdoor, metro, posters, cards, Website home pages, landing pages, inserts, and counter-toppers.

Hard Week?

This Weekend make it Jack's

Jack's Cafe

The Conversation Format

PERSUASIVE DIALOGUE

Description:

The conversation format is used to sell high-involvement products, services, and ideas. This proves to be very cost-effective as a customer is able to "converse" with a single informative ad with no assistance from a paid employee. Such ads earn the reputation as "24/7 salespersons," always ready and capable of closing the deal at a relatively low cost to the company.

When Used:

The conversation format is used with product offerings that demand explanation and/or require persuasion to sell. For example, the insurance industry relies heavily on personal sales, but when this is not possible or economically feasible due to tightening budgets, the conversation format provides an alternative that is relatively cheap and has the added benefit of reaching a much broader audience than is possible with one-to-one sales. The conversation format is also particularly useful for selling "the new thing," whether it consists of a radical, discontinuous innovation or the latest in a stream of continuous product changes. A picture of the product by itself is not enough. Copy is required to convince the customer that the altered or completely new product is worth the risk of trying. Because of its superior ability to persuade, this format may also be used for public relations crises where the customer demands explanation and needs to be reassured that the company's products are safe.

Copy/Image Balance and Execution:

The conversation format relies on copy to inform, interact, and persuade. A visual image may be used to reinforce the dialogue. Optional copy includes: headline, sub-heading, pack shot, and boxed price. Mandatory copy includes: body copy (the conversation), branding, and legally required information.

Media Used:

The conversation format may be used with print, Website home pages, brochures, landing pages, inserts, fax, cards, and counter-toppers. Due to its reliance on heavy copy, this format is not appropriate for outdoor and metro ads.

Have you heard the one about the lawyer...

You know, the one who has
been working on behalf of
the homeless since 1982?

Meet Brian
Attorney-at-Law.
No Joke.

At Rake Law, we help students set goals that go
beyond six-figure salaries and a new Porsche.

Visit us online or call us to see how you can begin
to help make justice happen.

The Humor, Sex, and Babies Formats

UNABASHED ATTENTION-GETTERS

Description:

When all else fails …. A well-known industry secret is that you can tell when the creative team ran out of ideas on ways to attract audience attention-the ad will have clear sexual connotations, use humor, or will include a picture of a baby (or a baby animal). Some products are logically connected to sex (condoms), humor (sit-coms), and babies (diapers). When used solely to attract attention, these three will be used even though there is no logical connection to the product (e.g., a picture of a baby used to sell motor oil or the classic buxom female draped over the hood of a car).

When Used:

These formats are used when advertisers believe that their ads lack attention-getting power. There is one caveat: Never should the attention-getting stimuli eclipse the product, as it did in the classic "Where's the Beef" campaign by Wendy's (in post-tests, most viewers wrongly believed the commercial was for McDonald's, not Wendy's). Ads that are too sexy, too humorous, or too cutesy run the real risk of creating attention at the expense of enhancing accurate comprehension and/or prompting positive consumer action. In other words, they risk preempting the real "star" of the ad, namely, the product.

Copy/Image Balance and Execution:

The format balance is moot: No holds are barred when it comes to the types of layouts the advertiser may choose for these ads. Execution-wise, advertisers understand that humor, sex, and babies work best when they reinforce the central message. When unconnected to the central benefit or promise, these formats serve to draw attention to themselves alone and, possibly, away from the product.

Media Used:

Attention-getting images work particularly well for outdoor and metro advertising where the time afforded to get a person's attention is seriously limited. But the beauty of these three is that they can be used in almost any advertising venue.

Tails - We Win

Bring Harold's Casino to Wisconsin
Vote ☑ YES on Prop. 9

The Stack Format

SYMMETRY AND SIMPLICITY

Description:

The stack format derives its name from its visual trademarks, which are two vertical stacks or bands, one consisting of visual images and the other, verbal copy. The visual stack typically appears on the right and the verbal stack on the left side of the ad field. The strength of this ad format lies in its sense of simplicity enhanced by balanced symmetry, the latter achieved by juxtaposing the two stacks side-by-side. Simplicity is achieved by using a generous portion of gutter space to surround both stacks, permitting the information in both stacks to "pop" and draw attention.

When Used:

The stack is used when advertisers believe that they have one or more strong visual images of the product. That said, sometimes even the best visual images by themselves fall short of being compelling without assistance. Verbal copy to the left of the stack fills this need, descriptively reinforcing the images. The compositional form of the verbal stack should be kept simple (no story, conversation, or copy-heavy description).

Copy/Image Balance and Execution:

The visual stack may take two forms: three different images or a single image repeated three times to reinforce the impact. No less than 80% of the ad field should be devoted to the two stacks. Of that eighty percent, 20% should be devoted to each stack separately, leaving 40% for white space. With the 20% left over, space should be given to headline and to a combination of: body copy, branding, price, pack shot, and legally required information.

Media Used:

The stack format offers a strong alternative for outdoor and metro as long as the verbal stack content is kept to a bare minimum. For example, by placing just three words stacked on top of each other that correspond to three visual images in a generous field of gutter space, the message is easily comprehended even when the viewer is speeding along at 80 mph. The stack also works for: print, Website home page, brochure, landing page, insert, and fax.

NEITHER RAIN NOR SLEET NOR DEAD OF NIGHT.

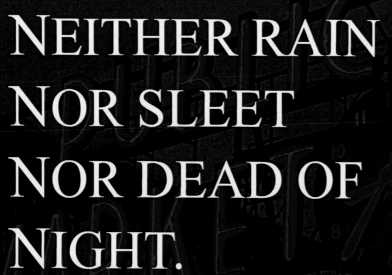

Hike Place Market
Seattle, WA
6AM to Midnight- 365

The Circus Format

CONTROLLED CHAOS

Description:

The circus format uses asymmetry to create a sense of enjoyment and lightheartedness. In the opposite way that strict lines and symmetry add formality and balance to an ad, with this format, unexpected lines and off-kilter angles are used to convey a sense of informality and even wackiness. The circus format leaves the audience with the idea that the consumption experience is something that will be enjoyable, even adventurous.

When Used:

The circus layout is used when there are lots of visual and verbal product stimuli from which to choose. Product inventory is on display in the circus format in appealing and eye-catching colors and lively descriptions. It works well with advertising for shopping malls, department stores, flea markets, large food buffets, cruise ships, casinos, fast-food restaurants, fairs, circuses of course, and other venues that offer a vast array of products in a "shopping-as-entertainment" setting. The circus format also works with single-line retail businesses, such as shoe shops and eyewear shops, where the merchandise line, albeit shallow, is broad and ripe for display. It is never used when the advertiser's intent is to communicate a serious message, such as might be the case with pharmaceuticals, law firms, investment companies, and insurance products.

Copy/Image Balance and Execution:

This is one of those "don't try this at home" formats that require a professional artist/designer to construct. The reason is simple: there is too much room for serious error when amateurs have a go at it. Good comedy is "organized spontaneity" according to many legendary stand-ups and the same is true here, with emphasis on the word "organized." Lines and angles invariably point the audience in a direction, and if they are not carefully positioned, it is very possible that they will usher the viewer right off the advertisement, possibly right into the lap of a competing advertisement.

Media Used:

The circus format works very well with print advertising, especially magazine ads and posters that are capable of using vibrant and rich colors. It is too visually complicated for outdoor and metro advertisements. It can work with landing pages and Web home pages as long as the intended effect is one of enjoyment and excitement. It is cautiously recommended for counter-toppers, fax, cards, inserts, and brochures because these are often used to quickly communicate a message (i.e., a deal), and by its complex nature, the circus format is not always quickly understood.

Delicious

Healthy

Flavorful

Fresh

Authentic

What more do you need?

Jacob's Platter
SANTA BARBARA, CA

The Stare Format

UP CLOSE AND PERSONAL

Description:

The strength of the stare format can be summarized in one word: engaging. By posing the model to look directly at the viewer, the advertiser is hoping to "get personal" with her/him. A staring model provokes the same feelings people have when they believe that someone is looking at them. It is deliberately used by the advertiser to unsettle the viewer. The stare format can also be confrontational (e.g., "isn't it about time you stopped avoiding those gray hairs"), and even titillating.

When Used:

The stare format can be sexually provocative and is often used to advertise "sin products," such as cigarettes, liquor, and condoms. It is sometimes used in men's magazines with ordinary products, such as health and beauty products, automobiles, jewelry, and cologne. It is primarily used in women's magazines to advertise health and beauty products, clothing, perfume, and jewelry. Copy often clarifies the advertiser's desired response. For example, with the very same picture, copy can elicit a sexual as well as a non-sexual response depending on what is written (e.g., a headline suggesting that the model is deep in thought, trying to find the right college).

Copy/Image Balance and Execution:

The model plays a central role in the stare format and consequently often consumes a large part of the ad field, taking up as much as 90% of the entire advertisement. A gigantic image of the model serves to intensify the provocative and engaging effects of the stare format and strengthens the possibility of establishing a personal connection with the viewer.

Media Used:

The stare format may be used in variety of media, including: magazines, outdoor, display, cards, fax, Website home pages, landing pages, inserts, and counter-toppers. To be effective, high resolution images are required and the advertiser should exercise caution before using the stare format in newspapers.

Satin
Dhal

Café India

The Tree Format
SIMPLE AND ITEMIZED

Description:

The tree format gets its name from its layout which consists of a vertical "trunk" with lateral "branches." The branches consist of verbal text that helps describe the image. The tree format combines the synergy of visual and verbal information, reflecting the advertiser's confidence in both to deliver a single compelling message about a new product or innovative feature. Therefore, the tree format is used only when advertisers believe they have a strong image and equally strong copy that, when combined, grab attention and communicate the promised benefits of using the product.

When Used:

The tree format is typically used with brand new products, product roll-outs, and continuous product innovations, visually displaying the new product (the trunk) and verbally "itemizing" its new and distinctive qualities (the branches). Completely new products are not welcomed by all consumers and one way to lower the risk of trial is to spell out exactly what's in the product. For example, the Big Mac in 1968 was not just a menu innovation but a product innovation that required explanation. Up until then, "a hamburger was a hamburger was a hamburger." The "two all-beef patties, special sauce, lettuce, cheese, pickles, onions on a sesame-seed bun" campaign advertised the Big Mac in a clever way by listing the ingredients, reinforcing memory for each by using a verbal cadence. Decades later, many are still able to precisely identify the ingredients of this legendary sandwich. Not all product innovations are completely new. When existing products receive minor alterations, the tree format permits the advertiser to display the product (such as toothbrush) with descriptions next to each change (such as a newly designed ergonomic handle).

Copy/Image Balance and Execution:

Audience attention is directed at the copy/visual display (the entire tree) by placing it in a large, white gutter space. The whole display will take up no less than 80% of the ad field. "Non-branch" copy will consume the remaining 20% and may include: headline, branding, price, and legally required information.

Media Used:

Product roll-outs are amenable to any media, but this particular format works best with: print, Web home pages, landing pages, cards, fax, counter-toppers, and inserts. Outdoor and metro can work as long as the verbal copy is left to a bare minimum, such as single or two-word branches.

EAT

GRIN

GRIP

Jacob's Platter
SANTA BARBARA, CA

The Copy Heavy Format
SERIOUS AND INFORMATIONAL (WITH IMAGE)

Description:

The copy heavy format provides detailed copy that addresses a single or a few issues related to the product. It is a good choice when the advertiser believes that the consumer needs and wants to be informed about particular aspects of the product before she/he can take a positive action toward the product.

When Used:

The copy heavy format is used extensively in industry and business-to-business advertising. Institutional buyers require complex information compared to ultimate (everyday) consumers because of the expense of the product, which may run into thousands of dollars. Consequently, they need information and lots of it before they make their decision to buy. Just as you would not expect to advertise a 69-cent bar of soap with a copy heavy format, neither would you expect to sell a $300,000 piece of machinery with a poster format consisting of a single image of the product and a 5-word headline. There are high-involvement consumer products (e.g., over-the-counter pharmaceutical products) as well as everyday products about which consumers demand lots of detailed information before buying (e.g., the nutritional content of some grocery items) and for these types of products, the copy heavy format may be appropriate. Finally, this format may be used in public relation crises where the company needs to reassure the public that their products are safe to consume. Used as such, this format may help change negative beliefs about and perceptions of the product.

Copy/Image Balance and Execution:

Body copy may constitute as much as 90% of the ad field. Other types of copy that may be used include: headline, sub-heading, price, branding, and legally required information. A small "stamp" shot of the product is often incorporated in the center of the ad field, just above or over the half-way mark. Advertisers use a small photo of the product or brand when they believe that, without it, there may confusion about the product/company identity.

Media Used:

The copy heavy format is most often seen in newspaper advertising because color quality is usually not that critical. Conversely, it is rarely seen in magazine advertising where advertisers pay a premium for high-resolution color options. It is never appropriate for outdoor and metro. It would rarely be seen on a Website home page; however, a link on the home page connected to a copy heavy landing page may be used. Copy heavy is rarely used for fax and counter-toppers; however, it may be useful for inserts and cards where the advertiser believes that the targeted consumer requires lots of detailed information to make a decision.

It's all in the news these days. What's going to be the next food that we won't be able to consume because it's carrying Salmonella or Mad Cow disease? With the recent soil contamination in Brazil, we wanted to give you the facts straight. Who are we? We are men and women just like you who love coffee. It is our passion and our livelihood. We are the United Association of Coffee Growers. We are committed to providing the freshest, affordable, and safest coffee beans in the world.

Image (c) daming, 2009. Used under license from Shutterstock, Inc.

Many companies tell you not to worry but that is not reassuring in today's world. We want you to have faith in our product. We have our experts working rigorously around the clock to make sure your coffee beans are safe.

All of our beans are selectively hand-picked by our workers. This means that only the best and ripe beans are picked. They are then sent to our testing facility, before they are to be processed. Our testing is rigorous. We hand sort through the beans after picking. Then a large sample is taken and tested for contaminants. If beans which are contaminated are found, another sample is taken to determine the extent of the contamination. Then the beans are sorted by a fan-driven winnowing system. This helps determine which beans will be sent to wet processing. We have three checkpoints the beans must pass to verify safety.

So far none of our beans have been contaminated. However, we believe by taking preventative measures now, we prepare a better future for our customers and ourselves. Our coffee beans have always provided you with the best cup of coffee. They have been there for you helping you through your hardest days. Our coffee beans will never give up on you, don't give up on them.

Brought to you by the United Association of Coffee Growers

The Editorial Format

SERIOUS AND INFORMATIONAL (WITHOUT IMAGE)

Description:

The editorial format is image-free advertising designed to offer detailed description for audiences highly involved in the product and buying process. The editorial is so named because it is easy to mistake it for a newspaper editorial or opinion piece. Consequently, some publishers require that the advertisers indicate at the beginning or end of the advertisement that it is, indeed, an advertisement and not an editorial opinion representative of the publisher's views.

When Used:

The editorial may be used for business-to-business and industry advertising (but at the risk of being uninspiring, if not boring). For all practical purposes, it is the preferred format when a company is experiencing serious problems related to their product and, as such, it is an effective tool for addressing a public relations crisis, such as tainted food or products that have injured or killed consumers.

Copy/Image Balance and Execution:

Because there is no visual material, composition decisions are relatively easy to make and determined mostly on how many columns of information are needed to create a pleasing, balanced, and informative display.

Media Used:

The editorial is mostly seen in newspaper advertising but may also appear in magazines if a product crisis is widespread. It is not appropriate for outdoor or metro advertising but may be used with fax advertising, especially when the target audience is composed of loyal customers whose fears need to be quickly quelled. A card or brochure campaign may also be used to address loyal customer concerns as well as the concerns of future, potential customers. On the company home page, consumers may be asked to click on a button that takes them to a temporary landing page that addresses the problems facing the company or the problems that they, the consumer, potentially face. It is not advised that the company allow an editorial format to visually dominate their home page.

It's all in the news these days. What's going to be the next food that we won't be able to consume because it's carrying Salmonella or Mad Cow disease? With the recent soil contamination in Brazil, we wanted to give you the facts straight. Who are we? We are men and women just like you who love coffee. It is our passion and our livelihood. We are the United Association of Coffee Growers. We are committed to providing the freshest, affordable, and safest coffee beans in the world.

Many companies tell you not to worry but that is not reassuring in today's world. We want you to have faith in our product. We have our experts working rigorously around the clock to make sure your coffee beans are safe.

All of our beans are selectively hand-picked by our workers. This means that only the best and ripe beans are picked. They are then sent to our testing facility, before they are to be processed. Our testing is rigorous. We hand sort through the beans after picking. Then a large sample is taken and tested for contaminants. If beans which are contaminated are found, another sample is taken to determine the extent of the contamination. Then the beans are sorted by a fan-driven winnowing system. This helps determine which beans will be sent to wet processing. We have three checkpoints the beans must pass to verify safety.

So far none of our beans have been contaminated. However, we believe by taking preventative measures now, we prepare a better future for our customers and ourselves. Our coffee beans have always provided you with the best cup of coffee. They have been there for you helping you through your hardest days. Our coffee beans will never give up on you, don't give up on them.

Brought to you by the United Association of Coffee Growers

This is an Advertisement

The Picture Window Format

A COMPELLING PROMISE

Description:

The success of the picture window format relies on identifying the most compelling promise the advertiser can make and then placing that promise in 45% or more of the ad field. By compelling, we mean that the content in the picture window by itself will compel the viewer to take a positive action toward the advertised product. The promise may be encoded visually or verbally.

When Used:

The picture window is extensively used in the "Big Four" of advertising photography: fashion, food, automobiles, and travel. The picture window format is flexible: what appears in the picture window can be either visual or copy. Compelling copy most often appears as a strong headline often in large, blocky, black letters. Against a white background that takes up over half of the ad field, the headline "jumps" off the page, making it virtually impossible to avoid. The viewer "gets it,"-quickly, and this is why the picture window is so popular in magazine advertising where researchers estimate that the typical reader spends less than two seconds viewing each advertisement. Writing headline that proposes a compelling promise is a task that goes beyond the scope of this book. In a nutshell, headlines that make a compelling promise do one of three things: 1) they promise to offer a solution to a problem the consumer hopes to solve (e.g., "where should I eat tonight?"); 2) they promise to offer a product that personally benefits the consumer (e.g., peace of mind, predictability, excellent price/value); 3) and/or they make promises that reflect the self-image of the targeted consumer (e.g., a loving spouse, someone with a discriminating tastes, a hard worker who deserves the best).

Copy/Image Balance and Execution:

The picture window by itself should not take up less than 45% or more than 90% of the ad field. It should end above or below the half-way mark, not exactly on the "50-yard line" of the ad field as this will result in uninspiring, if not boring, composition. Beyond the space taken up by the picture window, the ad should allow room to include: headline (which, if not in the picture window, should take up 15% of the ad field); body copy (which is optional and should take up 25% of the ad field); branding (which constitutes less than 5% of the field and may consist of a visual "stamp" of the company logo, storefront, the owners, or a product offering); legal requirements; and a subheading and pack shot (both of which are optional).

Media Used:

The picture window format is especially popular with magazines. They also work with: brochures, inserts, newspapers, posters, Website home pages, landing pages, counter-toppers, and fax. This format is not appropriate for outdoor and metro advertising if dense body copy is used. If using newspaper, the advertiser is urged to place copy, not image, in the picture window due to the poor color resolution of newspaper print.

What's Missing?

Le Beers

The Mondriaan Format

VISUAL FORMALITY

Description:

The name "Mondrian" is derived from the artist, Piet Mondriaan (1872-1944), who devised a style of painting that used a grid of vertical and horizontal black lines filled in with primary colors. To the right is a Mondriaan painting.

The Mondriaan style conveys an overall sense of balance and formality. The symmetry of a Mondriaan-style advertisement also sets a serious tone. This is not a humorous, lighthearted format that should be used, for example, with restaurants that want to appeal to an evening of family fun or to advertise impulse products, such as a candy and chewing gum. As one can see from the painting to the right, without a single letter of copy, the artist is able to convey a sense of culture, sophistication, and good taste.

© fat_fa_tin, 2009. Used under license from Shutterstock, Inc.

When Used:

The Mondriaan is used when the advertiser feels she/he has a compelling visual image, such as a photograph or illustration. It is a "natural" for expensive retail stores and cafés, but it can also be used by establishments that offer low-priced products and want to convey a sense of quality without high cost. Like an excellently designed package, the Mondriaan format can be used to "brand" a retail business, differentiate a business from its competitors, justify the price/value of the product and consumption experience, and "select out" the target customer.

Copy/Image Balance and Execution:

Design-wise, the Mondriaan format is relatively easy to produce and quite flexible. The advertiser designs a collection of rectangles (usually no more than four) of varying sizes with the purpose of filling in each with copy and/or visual images. Rectangle size can be used to draw primary attention to, for example, the beauty of a café offering by relegating a visual image of a dish to the largest rectangle.

Media Used:

The Mondriaan's strength is its visual display, and it may be used with nearly any media by the advertiser who wishes to convey a serious and formal tone. Print, Website home page, landing pages, inserts, brochures, fax, outdoor and metro advertising-the Mondriaan format works well with most any venue that enhances visual images and verbal copy.

For over 70 years the good citizens of Trieste in northern Italy have started their day with Illy.

Now its *your* turn.
Illyusa.com

The Story Format
ATTENTION-HOLDING

Description:

The story format uses a short narrative to accomplish two things: 1) pull the reader into the ad, and 2) direct the reader's attention to the promised benefit of using the product. It accomplishes these with the use of clever storytelling that may or may not relate directly to the product. In the former case, the objective is to describe a problem the consumer has or a mistake she/he has made because the advertised product was not used. The story may, for example, be about a car owner whose vehicle is shown broken down on the side of the road. In the ad story, the advertised product (e.g., a local mechanic's shop or a franchised auto parts dealership) emerges as the "hero" that would have been able to save the driver from encountering the problem had he purchased the advertised product. Another technique is to compose stories that do not directly relate to the product. These types of stories are used to raise curiosity (for example, the story causes the reader to ask "What does this story have to do with a good martini?") and hold attention. The goals with both types of stories are the same: to grab and steer the reader's attention to the promised benefits of using the advertised product.

When Used:

The story is used as a pointer device. Like a well-written comic strip, once the audience starts to read a really good story, they just have to finish it. The end of the story directs the consumers' attention and eventually "drops them off" at the promised benefit, such as a time-sensitive price deal. Sometimes, advertisers use the story format as default measure when there is no compelling visual of the product. The lack of a strong image may be related to the lack of good photography or illustration, but most often it is related to the fact that the product being advertised is not photogenic (e.g., a stick of gum), is visually uninteresting (e.g., bottled water), or is distasteful or aversive (e.g., the amber color of some beer and liquor products).

Copy/Image Balance and Execution:

A successful ad will employ the synergy of copy and visual to create a memorable lesson. Because the strength of the story format is the copy which tells the story, copy should dominate, taking up no less than 60% of the ad field. The visual serves to "punch-up" the story and reinforce its moral, and it should be given no less than 20% of the ad field. As a pointing device, the story may be placed in the top half and the visual in the bottom portion of the ad field, or the story and visual may be juxtaposed side-by-side.

Media Used:

Due to the amount of involvement demanded of the audience with this format, the story format is most often used in magazines and, to a lesser degree, in landing pages, fax, cards, and inserts and brochures-four venues that afford the space and time needed for the audience to read a story. It is never seen in outdoor and metro or on Web home pages. (It is a staple of TV and radio advertising in the form of story scripts).

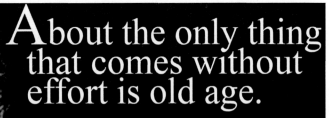

About the only thing that comes without effort is old age.

Why make it more of a battle then it has to be?

Meet Ralph, 67, retired Naval Lieutenant-Commander. He battled in Vietnam as a US Marine. With all that he has been through you'd think that growing old would be easy. It wasn't- until he found ARAP.

We take care of men and women who have been fighting the good fight all their lives. We fight your daily battles for you right on the home front so you have more time to enjoy the things you love. When it comes to quality care and outstanding benfits, you don't have to fight alone.

Call ARAP today.

The Silhouette Format

SUGGESTIVE AND NAUGHTY

Description:

The silhouette format uses shadows and indistinct lines, images, and angles to create a sense of mystery that implies risqué (but not tawdry, lecherous, or overly salacious) behavior. The blurriness of the image leaves the impression that the viewer is looking, undetected, at someone. Done well, the advertisement that uses the silhouette format can create a sense of arousal in the viewer not unlike the excitement felt by someone who witnesses private acts that are clearly not intended for "public consumption."

When Used:

"Sin products," such as cigarettes, alcoholic beverages, and condoms use the silhouette format in an attribution set-up (e.g., to imply that the reason the model in the ad is so successful with the opposite sex is because he drinks a particular brand of scotch). This format is best used with urbane and worldly audiences and may be geographically restrained; for example, what works in New York City may not work in Oklahoma City. An ad for the same product, say shampoo, may use a silhouette format in Playboy Magazine (e.g., an outline of a couple behind a steamy shower glass), but not in Good Housekeeping, where an image of a mother washing her child's hair would be appropriate. For this reason, the silhouette format should be used cautiously as it may provoke moral outrage, not just because of the sexual suggestiveness but also because of its attribution, cause-effect association between the consumption of the brand and the implied (usually illicit) outcome.

Copy/Image Balance and Execution:

Image is given a prominent spot in the silhouette format and copy is kept to a minimum. The reason: the image says it all. Copy-wise, the mere presence of the brand logo may be all the copy required. Often a pack shot is included (e.g., a bottle of gin) to aid the viewer in readily identifying the product on the store shelf, but this image should exist as little more than a small stamp and not be afforded visual dominance.

Media Used:

The silhouette format is quite flexible and may be used in outdoor, metro, print, Website home pages, landing pages, fax, counter-toppers, inserts, and cards. The media is not so much the issue as the placement of the ad which, as mentioned earlier, may provoke unwanted reaction in certain markets or particular media vehicles.

Our

Affair.

Emilie's Cafe
110 Park
Midtown

The Image/Copy Format
DETAILED PRODUCT DESCRIPTIONS

Description:

The image/copy format is an expanded version of the tree format which also uses a combination of image and copy. Like the tree format, advertisers use the image/copy format when they believe they have both strong copy and image available. Unlike the tree format, the image/copy format allows the advertiser to go into more verbal details about selected components of the product. The image/copy format also does not rely on a "trunk and branch" design to get its point across, permitting advertisers to describe more than a single product, something that is not possible with the tree format.

When Used:

The image/copy format works particularly well for retailers and industrial sellers who offer customers a broad inventory of items and who want to include a select number of those products in a single advertisement. The vast majority of advertising focuses on a single product. The focus on one thing only is not only standard but sound advertising practice which embraces "more is less" design technique. Nevertheless, there are times when advertisers wish to advertise multiple products in a single advertisement either because they believe it will be the most effective form of advertising or because of budgetary restraints. At such times, the image/copy format is the best choice for ad layout. The image/copy format can also be used to tease out details of a single product, such as a menu offering, which is deconstructed and its parts described.

Copy/Image Balance and Execution:

The ad field in the image/copy format can be very full-often taking up the entire advertisement with virtually no white space left over. The image may consist of a relatively small visual "stamp" followed by detailed verbal description. If multiple products are used, it is important that they all have a logical connection, what marketers call a "product constellation." For example, as spring approaches an appropriate constellation for a hardware store may include images and accompanying copy of a rake, bag of seeds, gloves, and fertilizer. For winter family meals, an advertisement for chili may use a constellation that includes a steaming hot bowl of chili accompanied by a bag of tortilla chips, shredded cheese, and fresh jalapeños.

Media Used:

Print ads and brochures work particularly well with the image/copy format when the verbal description is dense (both media are used when the target audience demands detailed description). When the copy and image are "lite," the options expand to include: outdoor, metro inserts, counter-toppers, Website home pages, landing pages, and fax-venues where simple and clean designs are most effective.

Zucchini

Eggplant

Carrot

Perfect

Dinner tonight was harvested from the Santa Ynez
Valley this morning.
Taste the local difference.

Jacob's Platter
SANTA BARBARA

The Pointer Formats
ATTENTION DIRECTORS

Description:

There are three pointer formats: size, comic strip, and visual cues. Many advertising formats that are discussed in this book, such as gaze motion, serve the purpose of directing the attention of the viewer to a particular item or piece of information. These three formats stand alone in that that their sole purpose is to steer attention to the most compelling element of the advertisement. The size format does this by presenting a single gigantic image of a product or model making it impossible to avoid. (See Exhibit 6 on page 68 for an example of the Size Format). The comic strip format accomplishes this by getting viewers involved in a story (the comic strip) that they can't stop reading until the final frame, the punch line, which just happens to be juxtaposed next to the intended object of attention. The visual cue does this through clever photography or illustration that uses visual components of the image to steer unsuspecting viewers to the object of attention.

When Used:

Advertisers often use pointing devices when they believe that the most compelling object of attention may otherwise go unnoticed or simply not receive the attention it deserves-and the results will be disastrous. For example, if a company nears the end of the quarter with share prices below what are expected, brand managers can attempt to increase sales quickly and dramatically by drastically cutting prices. However, even this tried-and-true method for sharply and dramatically increasing sales can fall short if the advertising fails to draw audience attention to the discount. Each format is used in distinct ways. The size format is used most often when there is a "big and beautiful" image of the product available. The comic strip format is used only when the "moral" or punch line of the comic strip has something to do with the benefit of using the product. And the visual cue is used when images are available that contain subtle pointers that are not likely to consciously register with the audience.

Copy/Image Balance and Execution:

The size format dominates the ad field-that's its purpose-and so copy is given little space. If the product shot does not include the brand or name, then this will need to be added, usually at the bottom-right corner. With comic strip formats, the strip acts as a horizontal pointer so placement is crucial. The rule is to place the object of attention, such as a discounted price or newly introduced label, next to the last frame of the strip. For visual cues, professional illustrators and photographers may be needed to create product shots embedded with pointers. The more visually complex the product (e.g., food), the more likely one will find embedded pointers; the more visually simple the product (a filing cabinet), the less likely one will find pointers and will, consequently, need to fabricate them using design techniques.

Media Used:

The size format is standard for outdoor and metro-a billboard that is 95% filled with the image of a juicy hamburger and just enough branding may be all it takes for a motorist to get off at the next exit. Comic strips are most often seen in print advertising, especially magazine ads. The visual cue layout offers a flexible format that can be used in a variety of media, including print, outdoor, metro, brochures, counter-toppers, fax, Website home pages, landing pages, cards, and inserts.

RENO

That's *My* Vegas

The Poster/Color Field Formats

COMPELLING COLOR VISUAL

Description:

Both the color field and poster formats use top-shelf professional photography or illustration to produce product shots that leave the viewer with one thing in mind: "I've got to have that!" Because the images are so clean and compelling, little or no copy is needed to explain or reinforce them. What is the difference between a color field and poster format? One thing: the color field is spread over two pages whereas the poster appears on one page.

When Used:

Both color field and poster formats work for any product that is visually aesthetic and superbly photographed or illustrated. It is no coincidence that the four industries that predominantly use advertising photography-fashion, food, cars, and travel-are the biggest users of these two formats. Historically, car manufacturers have used the color field format to introduce annual car rollouts in elaborate visual displays that may run 10 or more panels long as a magazine fold-out. Similarly, fashion advertisements in women's and fashion magazines display the newest styles and designs. In the past, these formats have been extensively used by the travel industry whose advertisers offer lush and enticing images of tourist destinations bathed in vibrant and appealing colors. Food advertisements that use the poster format are seen by thousands of travelers who, speeding down the interstate highway, suddenly feel the urge to pull off at the next exit in search of a sandwich like the one they just saw pictured on a roadside billboard.

Copy/Image Balance and Execution:

The photographic image or illustration may be given as much as 95% of the entire ad field. If the poster image is not branded, it is critical that the brand appear somewhere in the advertisement (typically in the bottom right-hand corner of the advertisement) as so little other explanation is offered otherwise. Headlines are kept to a single line. Boxed prices may be included, usually in the left and bottom half of the advertisement.

Media Used:

These formats are a natural for magazine advertising, but also may be used in outdoor, metro, Website home pages, landing pages, fax, cards, brochures, posters, counter-toppers, and inserts. Because of their reliance on high-resolution color, these two formats should not be used in newspaper advertising.

Discover Arizona.
Rediscover your inner kid.

The Gutter Space Format

IRRESISTIBLE CONTRAST

Description:

The gutter space format is distinctive from any other in that its strength lies not with what is on the ad field, but with what is not. This format uses a large area of unfilled white space (the gutter space) to draw maximum attention to the central object(s) of focus (a reverse gutter space uses white on black). Like trying to hide a large black object in a field of fresh snow, the viewer's attention is immediately and irresistibly drawn to the object-it cannot not be noticed. As such, the gutter space format is useful as a pointing device, directing the viewer's attention to an unusually good offer.

When Used:

This format is used when the advertiser believes that the claim being made is very compelling, such as an extraordinarily low price. It is an effective format for "limited promotional offers," and it can be particularly useful for "driving" customers to the store, the company Website, or an event when accompanied by a clear call-to-action, such as an expiration date or limited merchandise claim. It is commonly used by the airlines in the Sunday edition of national newspapers to draw attention to low fares for the week.

Copy/Image Balance and Execution:

Employing the principle of "less is more," as much as 90% of the ad field may be devoted to white space (or black space in the reverse gutter). The object of attention is typically placed in the top half of the gutter space, just above or below the half-way point. The space left over is used to display information that reinforces the object of attention and may include: headline, pack shot, instructions to get a deal, price, branding, and legally required information.

Media Used:

As a promotional piece, this format is difficult to beat and may be effectively used with cards, brochures, inserts, counter-toppers, and a variety of direct mail drivers. As a traditional advertising piece, this format works with: print, fax, outdoor, metro, Website home page, and landing pages.

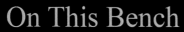

On This Bench
April 4, 1943

Two men made a decision
that changed the course of
world history.

Find out what was said.

The History Station
April 16 8PM EST

Glossary

Balance refers to the juxtaposition of elements in the advertisement which results in either a formal balance, characterized by symmetrical juxtaposition, or informal balance, seen when elements are in asymmetrical juxtaposition.

Big Idea refers to a single idea that encompasses the totality of the central promise and/or key consumer benefit being offered. It often appears in advertising as a slogan or headline. For the advertiser, the Big Idea acts as an organizing concept that keeps the creative team on track.

Black Glass is a photographic technique that shoots the product on black glass. It is often used with advertising for expensive products, such as watches and jewelry, and for products that want to project a high-class, expensive image. It is one of the most difficult shots to make and requires professional expertise to accomplish.

Call-to-Action refers to an incentive, usually monetary and limited by time, that compels the consumer to take an immediate action, as in "Buy in the next two days and receive an additional 20% off the suggested retail price."

Compelling means that the material prompts the consumer to take a positive action for the advertised product. Advertisers use a number of components to compel consumers to buy, including copy, visuals, prices, deals, and so forth.

Composition refers to the manner in which elements of the ad are placed in the ad field. It is an integral part of the advertising format as it specifies where visuals, copy, and other elements will be placed in the ad field.

Copy refers to the words used in the advertisement. In the case of radio and TV ads, copy refers to the script read by the actor or spokesperson.

Copy Platform states the message objectives and provides a creative blueprint that is consistent with the overall marketing plan. Normally, a copy platform will specify at least 10 things: the main problem the targeted consumer has with the product, the communication objective to meet that problem, a definition of the target audience, the tone of the advertisement, the key consumer benefit for using the product, the central promise being made to the consumer and support for that promise, the message idea statement (a summary of the key consumer benefits and promises), legal requirements, client requests, and "power copy" (or a slogan stated in 10 words or fewer).

Execution refers to how the advertiser intends to implement the ad message. Execution is accomplished through the use of copy (i.e., words) and art (i.e., visual stimuli). Strategy (what we intend to say to the audience) always precedes execution (how we intend to say it). The topic of this book, advertising format, addresses the question of advertising execution.

Illustration refers to non-photographic images rendered by an artist. One of the best-known American advertising illustrators was Norman Rockwell, whose clients included Heinz Catsup and Coca-Cola along with many other national brands.

Image refers to a photograph or some other visual representation, such as an artist's illustration, used in the advertisement. Images capture attention and are designed to compel the consumer to take a positive action (e.g., a professional shot of a new automobile may, by itself, be enough to compel the consumer to visit a local dealership).

Landing Pages also known as "white pages," refers to temporary cyber sites used as an alternative to the company Website. Landing pages allow advertisers to quickly and cheaply set up a site designed solely for their advertising campaign without having to hire expensive Web experts to alter the corporate Website. Landing pages are often designed as advertisements and may use standard advertising format and design. Landing pages are closely associated with pay-per-click campaigns which were created by Google in the mid-1990s.

Metro Advertising refers to ads that are placed on city transit, such as buses, cabs, and subways.

Photography (Advertising) refers to high-end commercial photography. Commercial photography is widely used in product advertising, especially in four areas: automobile, fashion, food, and travel. Commercial photographers may have completed as much as three to four years of education before turning professional.

Poster Advertising refers to advertisements that are placed in the public square such as on walls, fences, light posts, and kiosks.

Promise refers to the central promise made by the advertiser to the consumer, as in: "consume this product and we promise …." Most advertising emphasizes one promise (the primary claim) with one or two others (secondary and tertiary claims) that are not as strongly emphasized but important. As such, the promise defines the benefits to the consumer who uses the product. Less is more-the ideal is to be able to succeed with just a single compelling promise.

Strategy refers to what it is that the advertiser wants to say about the product. It uses the copy platform to accomplish this critical aspect of a campaign and may encompass 80 or even 90% of the entire advertising process.

Tone refers to the way the advertiser wants the viewer to feel as an outcome of viewing the advertisement. Lighthearted tones are enhanced by asymmetrical balance and serious tones are created with symmetrical balance.

Training Assignments
FOR CREATIVE ADVERTISING FORMATS

NAME _____ DATE _____

Assignment #1: Formats come and go, but these 25 have stood the test of time. Still, it might be interesting to look at formats that have been used in the past but are no longer with us. Check advertisements in general readership magazines, such as Newsweek, Time, or Life magazines that were published before 1960. Identify two formats that do not fit with any of the 25 written about here. Describe both formats and how they differ from any others explained in the book. Give the two formats two separate names and explain why you gave them those names. Describe what you believe are three strengths and three weaknesses of the two formats and identify one product, other than the one being advertised, that you believe works well with this format and explain why. Staple both ads to this sheet along with your responses.

Assignment #3: Identify the use of any of the 25 formats (your choice) for each of the following 5 media: a brochure, a card, a Website home page, an outdoor ad (shoot it with your phone or camera, print, and staple), and an insert. Below, identify the format used for each and staple a copy of each to this page.

Assignment #6: You are asked to kick off the first meeting of the creative team for the Crest toothpaste account. Create a PowerPoint presentation in which you explain three formats to your new ad creative team that you believe are strong candidates for the Crest print campaign. Make a hard copy of the presentation and staple it to this sheet along with the talking points you will use for the presentation.

Appendix

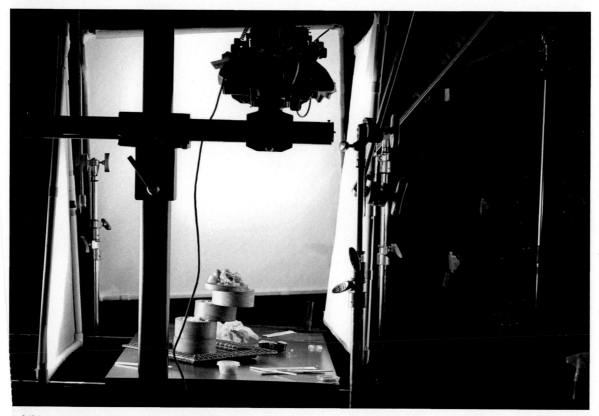

Exhibit 1: Behind the Shot—Circus/Jacob's Platter

Exhibit 2: Final Shot—Circus/Sushi Plates

Exhibit 3: Starting Shot—Marlboro

Exhibit 4: Final Shot—Marlboro

Exhibit 5: Branded Image Using Black Glass

Exhibit 6: Example of Size Format Used in Travel Advertising

Exhibit 7: Give it a Shot—Create Copy for 5 or 6 Different Products